Hillw
to C

Macgill

Seán Higgisson

The Eagle's Nest
Shehy Mountain
Tomies & Purple Mountain
Strickeen & Drishana
Cummeenapeasta Ridge
The Bone & Heaven's Gate
The Devil's Ladder
Coomloughra Horseshoe
Lough Acoose
Broaghnabinnia
Curraghmore
Brassel Mountain

Reprinted 2003

email: seanhiggisson@eircom.net

ISBN 0 9530194 1 1

Cover Photograph:
Lough Googh from Cummeenapeasta Ridge

Pen and ink drawings by Susan Keys

Also in the series:

Hillwalker's Guide to Mangerton

Hillwalker's Guide to County Cork

Special thanks to all who helped with the completion of the guide book.

Contents

Safety

Walk as part of a group, using an Ordnance Survey map, compass, and when possible, a guide. Have a good breakfast, make an early start and allow plenty of time for your walk.

Check the weather forecast before heading for the hills and be prepared for the possibility of cold, wet and windy conditions. If necessary cut your walk short, carefully retracing your steps and heading back the way you came. In the Kerry Mountains it rains on average 250 days a year. A light wind on the valley floor can turn to gale force on exposed ridges and it's 10°C colder at 1,000 metres than sea level.

Wear suitable clothing and proper hillwalking boots. Take sandwiches, boiled sweets and fruit, a flask in winter and plenty of liquids in summer. Also take a whistle, survival bag, torch and a small first aid kit.

Let someone know where you are going and what time you expect to be back. Remember to let them know that you have safely completed the walk. It is important to be off the mountain well before dark. Most accidents happen at the end of the day when you may be tired and careless. Leave a complete change of clothes in the car.

Maps

For all twelve hillwalks use the Discovery Series Ordnance Survey map No 78 Kerry, scale 1: 50,000.

The Sketch Maps

The orientation of the 12 sketch maps allows you to compare the maps with the landscape and avoid the need to turn the map during the initial stages of each walk.

The exact location of cliffs and other dangers can only be hinted at in the sketch maps and should not be regarded as a substitute for the Ordnance Survey maps, where their location is shown in more detail and accuracy.

Note

Some of the mountain peaks named in the guide book are taken from other guide books and are not used in current Ordnance Survey maps. These peaks are named with the corresponding height in metres.

Access to Farmland and the Hills

Farmland is private property and access is only available with the goodwill of the landowner. Entrants do so at their own risk and are obliged to take all necessary steps to ensure their own safety. They are also responsible for any damage they may cause to property or livestock.

Respect farmland and the rural environment. Take care on country roads, keep children under control, avoid making any unnecessary noise and please take your litter home with you.

Where possible use way-marked trails, gates and stiles. Avoid damage to fences and walls. Leave gates as you find them. Respect wildlife, guard against fires, especially near forests, and report any damage you may have caused to the landowner.

Do not enter farmland with your dog or interfere with crops or livestock or block farm entrances with your car. Remember, warning signs are there for your own protection. Your presence can cause stress to the animals and they can be dangerous.

Introduction

I hope you enjoy completing the walks and experience some of the wonders I savoured while compiling them. These twelve walks are on the whole more challenging than my previous guide book, *The Hillwalker's Guide to Mangerton*, and are intended for the seasoned hillwalker.

For the all year round hillwalker every season has its own attraction. During the summer months take advantage of the long days and relax beside some remote mountain lake. In winter have fun trudging through ankle-deep snow or watch dry powdery snow being held aloft by a whirlwind and flurry around the hills in a dervish dance.

While walking in the hills you might see large native Red Deer and smaller white-tailed Japanese Sika Deer near Coomclochan below Shehy Mountain, hares and foxes in the Hag's Glen near Meallis, mink in the Black Valley and wild goats near Lough Duff. It is common to hear ravens 'Kroking' noisily over the ridges of Cruach and to see red grouse in the high heather near Lough Eighter. Peregrine falcons soaring over Tomies Wood and osprey on Muckross Lake in early summer are a rarer sight. It is fun to watch trout jumping in Lough Callee and small fish swimming in the clear water of Gearhameen River above the waterfall and Lough Reagh.

For colour in the hills you have yellow furze, or gorse, from June to September, purple bell heather from July to September white bog cotton in late July and orchids in flower from June to August. In autumn the browns of the landscape are a delight and a feast for the eyes.

On cloudy days a shaft of sunlight can race across a valley floor like a heavenly searchlight. Towards sunset on misty days watch for the rare and mysterious brocken spectre and glory, when the sun casts your shadow in a rainbow on the mist. Mountain peaks can form a string of islands during an equally rare temperature inversion when cloud is trapped below. Watch mountain sheep negotiate inaccessible places and mountain peaks draw clouds out of clear blue skies.

Over the years an unplanned network of paths has developed through the hills from the constant tramping of mountain sheep and human feet. You will use this network on most of the walks but not all. For this reason hillwalking in Ireland can be hard work. It's a struggle to climb through knee-deep heather, long grass and ferns or to cross open bog with the peat clinging firmly to your boots.

History, Mythology and Folklore

The mountains of Kerry were formed 300 million years ago by a great uplifting and folding of the earth's crust. Many intervening periods of glaciation sculpted the sandstone hills into their present form. The warm epoch that we are in now started 10,000 years ago and the land has slowly re-forested itself, laying down successive layers of peat and bog. Between the start of early agriculture in 3000 BC and AD 1750 the forests were cleared and replaced with a field system of agriculture. Some half-buried old tree trunks are still visible in the open bog of the Hag's Glen.

There is evidence of past habitation in remote areas going back over three thousand years. Of interest is the abundance of standing stones, stone circles and stone rows, the remnant of a stone age Neolithic past. More mysterious is the rock art near Ballaghbeama Gap, consisting of a shallow hollow and a series of scarred rings. You will find a wealth of other such sites marked in the Ordnance Survey maps.

You may also come across old potato beds, derelict cottages and dry stone walls, a legacy of famine times when the population of the country was much higher than now. Observing ferns, bracken and heather reclaim unattended fields I have no doubt any mark we may leave on the landscape is only temporary and nature will reclaim all in the end.

In our past there was a rich belief in an underworld inhabited by fairies and leprechauns, who interacted with mortals for good and evil in myth and legend. The High King of Ireland's standing army, 'The Fianna', protected the country from invasion and hunted wild deer near Derryfanga, north of Lough Acoose. From the summit of Carrauntoohil you can clearly see the peninsula of Inch strand, where the fairy Niamh took the young Oisin on a white horse across the sea to Tír na nÓg, the land of eternal youth. Returning home after 300 years he fell from his horse while trying to pick up a boulder and immediately turned into an old man. Before he died he related the legends of 'The Fianna' to Saint Patrick.

The Hag 'an Cailleach', a powerful Celtic goddess, a builder of mountains, lives on in the Hag's Glen and the Hag's Lake. The serpent 'an Pheist' represents an evil force and the name lives on in Cummeenapeasta Ridge and Lough.

Choosing Your Walk

Choose your walk with care and have regard to its grading, the estimated time for the walk, the length in kilometres and the total ascent in metres. Ensure that it is within your capabilities. If in doubt try one of the moderate walks first before you proceed to the strenuous and challenging ones.

Your level of fitness and the number of breaks you have during the walk will determine how long it will take. The walks are listed in order of severity below.

The easy walks should not be a problem to anyone, as there is little if any climbing involved. The strenuous walks are generally longer then the moderate ones with steeper climbs. The challenging walks require a head for heights and a willingness to use your hands as you scramble your way to the ridges.

Two Easy Walks

1 The Eagle's Nest	9–10
9 Lough Acoose	21–32

Three Moderate Walks

4 Strickeen & Drishana	21–22
7 The Devil's Ladder	21–28
12 Brassel Mountain	37–42

Three Strenuous Walks

2 Shehy Mountain	9–12
3 Tomies and Purple Mountain	9–14
10 Broaghnabinnia	37–38

Four Challenging Walks

5 Cummeenapeasta Ridge	21–24
6 The Bone and Heaven's Gate	21–26
8 Coomloughra Horseshoe	21–30
11 Curraghmore	37–40

Shehy, Tomies and Purple Mountain

This is a small compact group of hills separating the rugged Reeks in the west from the gentler Mangerton Mountain range in the east. Walks 1 and 2 lie within Killarney national park and represent a chance to see some of the 600 native red deer in the wild. Tomies Wood abounds with thick spongy mosses, holly, sessile oak trees, rhododendrons and birdsong. From Shehy Mountain you have an unrivalled view of Killarney and her many lakes. Purple Mountain derives its name from the colour of the sandstone rock and not from the abundant purple bell heather on its slopes. Tomies Mountain towers over the entrance to the Gap of Dunloe and the mound of stones on the summit once marked the burial site of a great Kerry chieftain.

1 The Eagle's Nest

An easy 5 hour, 7 kilometre walk through woodland paths and marshy open country, followed by a stiff 200-metre climb to the summit of the Eagle's Nest. This remote, beautiful and seldom visited area of the national park was once a popular site for nesting eagles.

2 Shehy Mountain

This strenuous 7 hour, 12 kilometre hike starts with a pleasant stroll through Tomies Wood, followed by a severe scramble to the top of Shehy Mountain. The 800 metres of climb are well rewarded with a fine ridge walk and many contrasting views of the valleys below.

3 Tomies & Purple Mountain

This strenuous 6 hour, 13 kilometre walk starts with a steep 500-metre ascent through long grass and heather. It is rewarded with fine views from Tomies Mountain of the Gap of Dunloe and from Purple Mountain of the Black Valley.

I The Eagle's Nest

P–1

From the car park take the tarmac path into the woods for Dinish Island and cottage. On past the tall pine trees, the path meanders beside Muckross Lake to a clearing on the left which provides the first clear view of the Eagle's Nest. Later to your right there is a view of the arched Brickeen Bridge which separates Muckross Lake from lower Lough Leane. Further on, take the path to your left through the woods, follow the red posts and the wire mesh-covered sleepers to the old Weir Bridge and the meeting of the waters.

1–2

Cross the bridge and head upstream. Now climb the small hillock before you. From here you can see Shehy Mountain and Glena Wood to the north-west, the Eagle's Nest and Cahnicaun Wood to the south-west and Torc Mountain to the south-east. Head south-west, keeping to the higher ground and skirting the lower boggy areas until you reach the small lake. Approaching the Eagle's Nest, plot the route of your assent well away from the sheer cliffs. Cross the stream near a large boulder and a small copse of trees.

2–3

Continue on through the tussocks of long grass. Head south-south-west and climb the steep grassy slope, stopping to take in the views behind you. Take your time skirting the bluffs of rocks as you ascend. Higher up you reach a line of trees. Head south, climbing steeply through the long grass. At the ridge the ground levels out and a small square rock offers a welcome seat and a view of Killarney's Upper Lake and Cahnicaun Wood. Descend eastward down the centre of the spur past the holly and oak trees until you arrive at the Eagle's Nest. The area is well named, with steep cliffs on all three sides. During the summer months keep an eye out for the small motorboats in the Long Range Lake below.

3–2

Retrace your steps to the oak and holly trees. Continue your ascent up the centre of the spur until the ground levels out and you reach the small square rock again. Head north for the trees and descend north-eastwards to the small lake below. Watch the terrain and contour around difficult areas and proceed with care. Head for the large boulder on the far side of the stream beside a copse of trees.

2–1–P

Make your way through the tussocks of long grass. Cross the stream and climb the boulder for a brief rest. Head north-eastwards for the edge of the lake and skirt the boggy areas on the surrounding higher ground. Carry on until you reach the river and the Old Weir Bridge.

Cross the bridge and follow the path to Dinish Cottage for a cup of tea before returning your car.

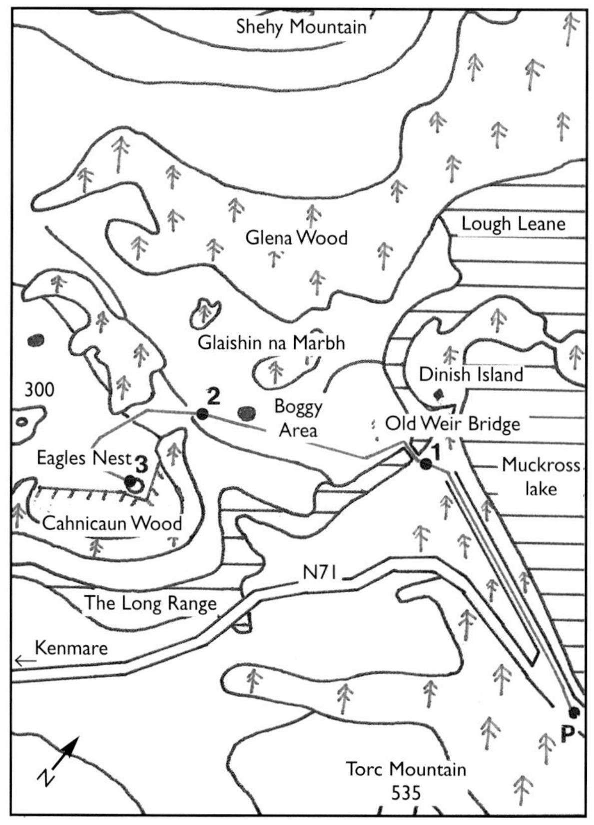

Easy; 5 hours; 7 kilometres; 200-metre ascent

2 Shehy Mountain

P–1

Take the path for Tomies Wood through the farmyard to the entrance of Killarney National Park. At the fork near a large boulder take the right-hand path, up a gentle incline through the woods. Cross the river by the stepping stones and continue along the path. There is open hillside on your right and, on your left, a fine panorama of Lough Leane from Ross Castle in the north-east to the mountains of Mangerton in the south-east. Continue along the path until you see a solitary rock in the hill above and the remains of some old fencing on your right.

1–2

Climb beside the old fence posts into the hills and further along to where the bog has slipped away to reveal a stony undersoil. Now climb to the newer fencing on the higher ground. Study the hill and plot your ascent to the summit of Shehy Mountain with care. The steep ground is entirely covered in heather and grass, offering firm footing and good hand holds. Zigzag and scramble your way to the top. Soon the ground levels out and the vista of Killarney from Shehy Mountain is unsurpassed. The summit of Shehy Mountain is seldom visited and you may be lucky enough to have the mountain to yourselves.

2–3

Proceed in a south-west direction up the centre of the ridge. At 632 metres take in the view of Killarney's Upper Lakes on your left and Coomclochan to your right. As you continue to climb, a higher peak of 762 metres towers overhead. Above 600 metres the thick heather gives way to a flat landscape of loose rock and sea pinks (thrift). At the third cairn, head north-north-west for the col between Purple and Tomies Mountain. Continue on until you reach the small cairn on the ridge overlooking the Gap of Dunloe. To the west the Macgillycuddy Reeks and Cummeenapeasta Ridge are dominant. Head north for the summit of Tomies Mountain and its distinctive shelter of loose stones.

3–P

From Tomies Mountain head east, descending through the steep heather, grass and loose rocks to the 682-metre mark. Continue your descent north-eastwards through the grass and stones to the small path below Gortadirra. From Gortadirra descend north-eastwards through the heather and long grass. Keep your eyes open for a place where the wood is thin and you can reach the path with ease.

Head north-west and retrace your steps back along the path to the entrance of Killarney National Park and your car.

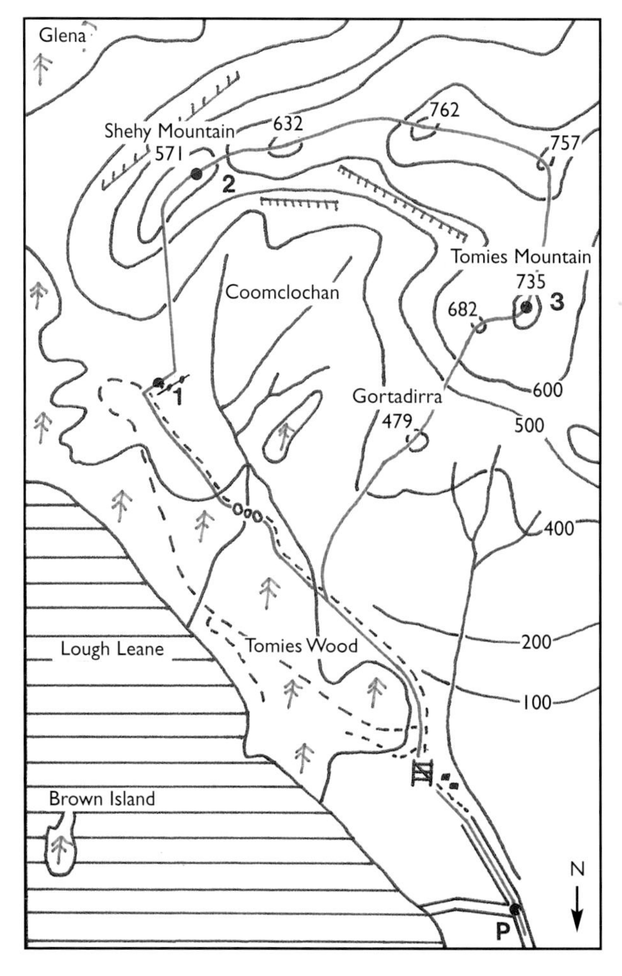

Strenuous; 7 hours; 12 kilometres; 800-metre ascent

3 Tomies & Purple Mountain

P–1

From the car park head north along the road to the craft shop, cross over the bridge and go through the tubular gates on your right. Continue on along the path towards the hill until the road levels out. Ahead of you is Lough Leane, with the golf course on your left. Below to your right is a green barn and tubular gate. Beyond the gate, climb through the long grass and heather to the fence in the hill above. Head for the corner of the field and climb through the ferns to cross into open hillside beyond.

Now head south, climbing through the long grass, ferns and heather to the 568-metre mark. The ground gets steeper as you ascend. Soon it levels out to reveal your first view of Tomies and Purple Mountain. To your right is the Gap of Dunloe and the Macgillycuddy Reeks beyond.

1–2

Head south-east for the col at the base of Tomies Mountain. Now a steep ascent of 200 metres through heather and loose scree will leave you breathless and elated at the summit of Tomies. The summit of Tomies Mountain is quite distinct, with its makeshift stone enclosure. Head south and stay well away from the steep cliffs to your left and right. At this height all the heather and grass are short and the path down the centre of the plateau is well defined. As you climb again the ridge narrows to reveal a steep precipice on your right. Near the summit is the first of three small cairns and a failed stone enclosure. The third cairn marks the summit of Purple Mountain (832m).

2–3

There are great views from the summit of Purple Mountain into the Black Valley and the Macgillycuddy Reeks beyond. From here you descend south-south-west through loose rocks, down the spur towards Glas Lough. The path becomes more apparent as you descend. Listen carefully and you will hear the clip clop of the jarvies' horses as they trot through the Gap of Dunloe during the summer months. Follow the fence down to Glas Lough.

Continue your descent to where the stream leaves the lough, beside the remains of the old stone wall and fence. Further along keep your eyes open for a path and the remains of an old fence on your right. This will bring you westward to the road and the Head of the Gap.

3–P

Follow the road north to Black Lough. The Gap narrows as you descend to Lake Auger and Cushnavally Lake. Continue on past Black Lake and Lough Coosaun to your car.

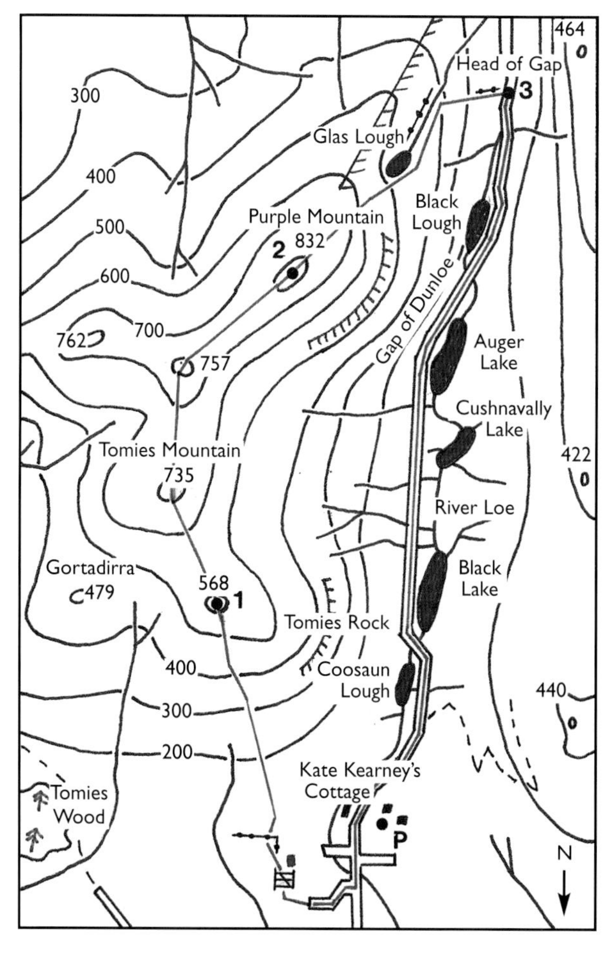

Strenuous; 6 hours; 13 kilometres; 900-metre ascent

Walk 1 The Eagle's Nest as seen from Torc Mountain

Walk 2 View of Killarney and Lough Leane from Gortadirra

Walk 3 View down to Glas Lough and the Gap of Dunloe

Walk 4 View of Tomies Mountain from Drishana

Walk 5 Lough Callee, Lough Gouragh, the Hag's Glen and Carrauntoohil from Cummeenapeasta Lough

Walks 7, 8, 11 The metal cross marking the summit of Carrauntoohil

Carrauntoohil

I saw the summer sun go down behind the sea,
And o'er the pale moon grow a golden light,
From lonely Carrauntoohil's topmost height
Towering aloft in cloudless majesty;
The serried hills beneath seem in the night
Like billowy ocean, heaving in its might
And turned to stone; while far as eye can see
The lengthening shadows o'er the surface flee
Around, each crag and jutting fragment tell
The name and features of the bedlam old,
Potent in herbs and versed in many a spell
Who dwelt unblest within her mountain hold
Oh blame not if each shadow as it fell
Seemed the weird phantom of the haunted dell.

Thomas Gallwey 1871

Macgillycuddy's Reeks

The range is extremely rugged with fine knife-edged ridges, high cliffs and fast-running rivers. Most of the peaks being over 700 metres in height escaped the glacial erosion visible on the lower slopes during the last Ice Age. The challenge of the scrambles and narrow ridges on walks 5, 6 and 8 make for an exhilarating day in the hills. These three walks should only be attempted by experienced hillwalkers on the finest of days or when accompanied by an experienced guide. The original timber cross on the summit of Carrauntoohil once boasted a set of lights. Unfortunately they did not survive the first winter storm. In 1976 the local community replaced the timber cross with a more durable metal one. In winter it is regularly hit by lightning, giving the surface a black and charred appearance.

While flying at night from Morocco to England in December 1943 an American C47 sky train crashed in the Reeks. The crew failed to take a course correction off the coast of Portugal and later mistook the Dingle Peninsula, with its high mountains, for the flat landscape of Cornwall in south-west England.

By now, flying blind, lost and seriously running low on fuel, they tragically crashed into the screed slope below Cummeenapeasta Ridge above the lake. A damaged wing submerged in the lake, but clearly visible from the ridge above, is the only remnant of the plane or its cargo of bicycles for the D-Day landing in Normandy during World War Two. There is a memorial plaque at Cronin's Yard to the five servicemen who died in the crash and to the climbers who lost their lives in the Reeks.

On Cruach More you will find the grotto, built single-handedly by Tom Sullivan in the mid-seventies. For three summers he laboured day and night to bring mortar gravel and water from Cummeenapeasta Lake to the ridge to build the monument. Sadly even a remote and beautiful area like this is not free of vandals and two of the last three statues have disappeared without trace. It is hard to imagine anyone living in the Hag's Glen on a permanent basis, but after the famine in 1850, when the landlords increasingly evicted their tenants, at least six souls lived in this remote, inhospitable but most beautiful of Glens.

4 Strickeen & Drishana

This moderate 6 hour, 13 kilometre walk through open bog includes 750 metres of climb with fine views of the Reeks in the west and the Black Valley to the south.

5 Cummeenapeasta Ridge

This challenging 7 hour, 10 kilometre knife-edged ridge walk with 900 metres of climb has one severe scramble and splendid views down to the Black Valley.

6 The Bone & Heaven's Gate

This challenging 7 hour, 12 kilometre ridge walk has 860 metres of climb. The ridge is wide and you can amble along at a leisurely pace taking in the scenery. The descent down through Heaven's Gate is spectacular, but you must be careful and stay with the path at all times.

7 The Devil's Ladder

This moderate 6 hour, 12 kilometre walk with 900 metres of climb is by far the most direct and straightforward approach to Carrauntoohil. Also known as the tourist route it is ideal for those who want to get to the summit and down again as quickly as possible.

8 Coomloughra Horseshoe

This is a challenging 7 hour, 11 kilometre, extensive ridge walk with 1,300 metres of climb over three Munros. From the summit of Carrauntoohil careful consideration must be given before you proceed out along the Beenkeragh Ridge and it should only be attempted by those comfortable with heights and sheer drops and willing to use their hands. If you have any doubts, retrace your steps to Caher.

9 Lough Acoose

This easy 3 hour, 6 kilometre stroll is ideal for those lazy days when the thought of another climb is just too much.

If you're lucky to complete the walk on a calm day, the reflection of the Mountains in the still waters of Lough Acoose is just magical.

4 Strickeen & Drishana

P–1

From the car park head south into the Gap of Dunloe. After five minutes take the path on your right beside the signpost for the Climber's Inn and the hills. Climb the zigzag path, stopping to take in the view of the Gap below. The path levels off near a small cairn of stones and Strickeen raises its head above the surrounding bogland. Head south-south-west over the flat bog. There are fine views of the Macgillycuddy Reeks to your right and the distinct shapes of Tomies and Purple Mountain to your left. As you slowly ascend, negotiate the bog banks with care until you reach a pile of loose stones near the base of the East Peak (731m).

1–2

Now you have a steep 250-metre ascent through heather and long grass. Skirt the bluffs of rock and negotiate a few false peaks before you finally reach the distinctive stone-crafted cairn on the summit of the East Peak, 731m. To the west is Cruach More and, beyond, the magnificent Macgillycuddy Reeks. To the south is the mysterious Black Valley. Head south-eastwards, descending slowly through the short heather and grass to the col below. Now climb again to Cnoc na Tarbh (655m), the hill of the bull, with its generous scattering of larger boulders is well named.

2–3

Head south, down along the spur, staying well away from the steep cliffs to your left and right. Continue your descent until you reach Drishana. From here you can see the Gap road to the east and the Black Valley to the south. Continue south down to the fence and then follow it eastward into the Gap. As you descend, the fence will end above a sheer outcrop. Contour carefully around this obstacle until you meet the fence again. Now continue your descent beside the fence until you reach the Head of the Gap.

3–P

From the Gap, follow the road north to Black Lough, where the last wolf in Ireland was shot in the eighteenth century. The Gap narrows as you descend to Lake Auger. Stop to take in the scene before you. Near Lake Cushnavally you can make echoes rebound from the surrounding hills. Towering overhead to your right are Tomies and Purple Mountain. You now approach the Black Lake, where legend has it that St Patrick drowned the serpent. Cross the bridge over the river Loe, continuing on past ink-black Lough Coosaun to your car.

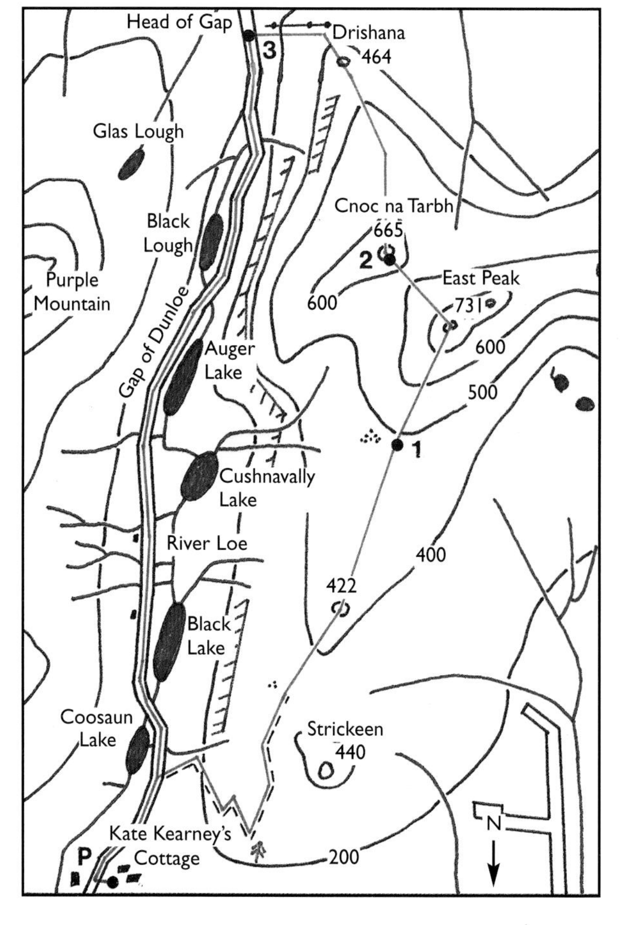

Moderate; 6 hours; 13 kilometres; 750-metre ascent

5 Cummeenapeasta Ridge

P–1

Take the path beyond the gate. Go over the bridge and stream until the landscape opens out. Continue on to the river and up the left bank to the small timber gate and fence.

1–2

Head south across open country, climbing steadily through the boulder fields towards the ridge separating the high peaks of Cruach Mór and Lackagarriv. Ascending through the boulders the ground gets progressively drier and steeper until you arrive at Lough Cummeenapeasta. Take in the view of Lough Callee, Lough Gouragh and Carrauntoohil to the west. From the Lough climb up the centre of the spur to the ridge on your right. There is a severe drop on your left and the craggy profile of the Bone to your right. As you climb, the ascent gets steeper, so stay with the grassy areas or use your hands to scramble over the rocks. Study the stark profile of Cummeenapeasta Ridge and look for the path on your left near the summit of Lackagarriv (988m).

2–3

The narrow elusive path meanders along the ridge to your right and left. Be prepared to clamber over rocks, using your hands, or walk on high ridges with precipices on both sides. On the more difficult sections look for the more defined path further down the side of the ridge. At the lowest point of the ridge, with the sun sparkling in Lough Googh, the ground rises steeply to Foilnabrechaun (939m). From here you can clearly see the submerged wing of the plane in Lough Cummeenapeasta and evidence of folding in the rocks. Stay with the path and continue to inch your way across the ridge to the fine stone-crafted grotto on Cruach Mór (932m).

The going gets easier as you head eastward down the ridge. There are fine views to your right of Kenmare Bay, with Purple Mountain directly ahead and the two small lakes to your left. Continue on across the fence, then climb again before descending to the col above the lakes.

3–1–P

Since the initial steep screed appearance of the gully looks dangerous and forbidding, it is better to progress a little further to the grass-covered slope, where you can descend slowly to the rocky outcrop on your right for an unbroken view down the gully to the small lakes below. As the descent is very steep, your progress will be slow but steady, so take your time. On reaching the base of the gully the ground levels off near a pleasant green oasis. Stay with the stream and continue on through the rocky outcrop to the first of the two small lakes.

Head west and climb to the high ground between the two lakes. Ascend to the ridge for an evening view of Carrauntoohil. Cross the fence and stream, head west-northwest, across open country and bog, until you arrive at the fence and timber gate. Follow the river to the path, which will take you back to Cronin's Yard and your car.

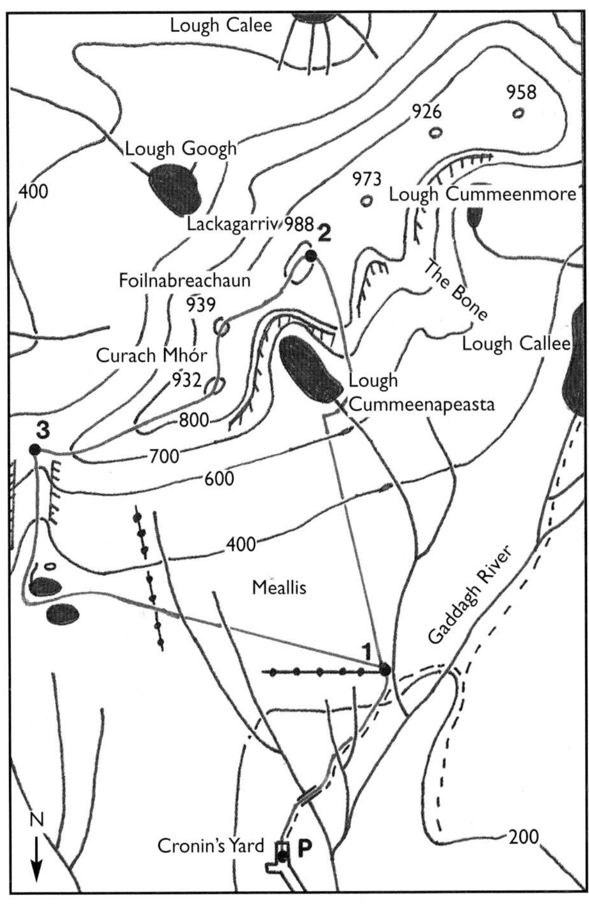

Challenging; 7 hours; 10 kilometres; 900-metre ascent

6 The Bone & Heaven's Gate

P–1

From Cronin's Yard take the path through the gate and over the bridge and the small stream. To your left is the high ridge of Cruach and in the middle distance a green ridge running from right to left will lead your eye to the Bone and its distinctive rugged appearance. Continue along the cobbled path to the river. Cross the river and climb to the bank on the far side. Then ascend to the ridge and on through the orange gate, and cross the bog to a cluster of small boulders.

1–2

Head south up the centre of the ridge, following the line of old metal fence posts and the remnant of a stone wall. Continue on beside the stream, past the lone tree and on to a distinctive large square boulder. Contour westward below the scree-strewn slopes of the Bone. Now climb and scramble your way up the craggy spur of the Bone to the ridge of Cruach. Keep Lough Cummeenmore in sight until you reach the small cairned summit of Moylaun Bwee (973m).

2–3

Head south-west on the path down the centre of the ridge, with severe drops to the right and left. Stay with the path and the cliffs until you arrive at Ballaghnageeha (926m) and on to Foilnagower (958m) and the small cairn. On no condition should you drift away from the ridge or the path. Descend along the path to the col, where you can see the spectacular waterfall above Lough Reagh in the Black Valley. Cross the fence and continue your ascent until the ridge levels off. Look for the path to Heaven's Gate between the Devil's Ladder and the waterfall above Lough Gouragh. With Lough Curraghmore and Broaghnabinnia on your left continue along the path on the ridge to the col above the Devil's Ladder.

3–4

Head north to a large outcrop of rocks to the right of the cairned path for Carrauntoohil. The path contours around the hill near a small cairn of stones on a narrow ledge in the middle of a screed slope, with Carrauntoohil on your left and sheer precipices to your right.

Further on, with high bluffs of rock on your left, take in the view down to the Hag's Glen. Continue on past the cascade until you arrive at the gap between two rocks,'Heavens Gate'. Descend the eroded path to arrive at the Mountain Rescue hut in the middle of a green hillock. Away to your left water cascades spectacularly from Looking Glass Lake.

Continue east-north-east from the hillock and make for the path on the far side of the stream. Cross the stream and join the path, contour around the hill and slowly descend towards the glen below. Cross the stream and pick up the path on the far side then continue down through the boulders to Lough Gouragh.

4–P

Head east-south-east for the path through the Hag's Glen. Cross the river and continue on the path. Then cross the river Gaddagh near a small copse of trees. Now follow the path on the far bank back to Cronin's Yard.

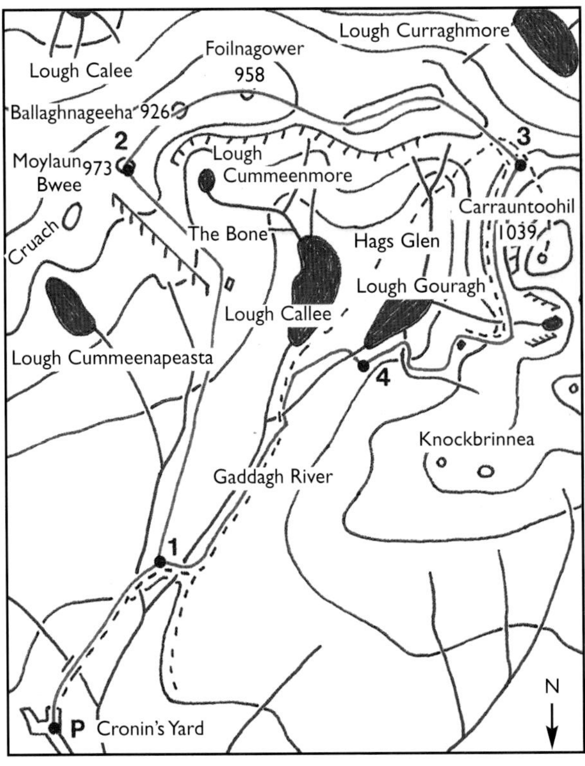

Challenging; 7 hours; 2 kilometres; 860-metre ascent

7 The Devil's Ladder

P–1

Take the path beyond the gate. Go over the bridge and the small stream until the landscape opens out. Continue on the path beside the dry stone wall with the magnificent ridge of Cruach high on your left. The landscape is bare of trees with lots of boulders; the grass is kept tightly cropped by the hardy mountain sheep. Cross the stream and continue along the path until you reach the river Gaddagh. Go through the gate, cross the river and climb to the trail on the far bank. Continue along the trail to the Hag's Tooth. The Devil's Ladder becomes more apparent to the left of Carrauntoohil, with the cross on the summit clearly visible.

1–2

Crossing the river you can clearly see the knife-edged ridge connecting Beenkeragh and Carrauntoohil. Soon you will arrive at Lough Callee and later its twin, Lough Gouragh, comes into view. Continue on through the Hag's Glen to the base of the Ladder, which is strewn with loose wet scree. In winter it can be dangerous, when the water freezes and the rocks are slippery. You can rest on the rocky outcrop halfway up. From here the Ladder gets progressively steeper, so you will have to use your hands to clamber over the rocks when the gully narrows. Here the erosion is at its worst and you can physically see the change from one year to another.

2–3

Before progressing, take in the scenery, as the summit of Carrauntoohil is often covered in mist and the view from here can be disappointing. To the south, Broaghnabinnia stands sentinel watching your ascent. Head north-west until you pick up the cairn-strewn path, which will take you to the summit of Carrauntoohil. Touch the cross for luck and stop for lunch.

On a clear day the view from Carrauntoohil is breathtaking. To the north are the Slieve Mish Mountains on the Dingle Peninsula; to the east the Galty Mountains in far-off Tipperary; to the south-west Kenmare Bay; to the north-west Inch Strand and Rossbeigh.

3–2

From the summit head south along the cairn-strewn path to the col above the Devil's Ladder.

2–1

Care is needed when descending the Ladder. Take time to stop and appreciate the view you missed on the way up.

1–P

Follow the path out through the Hag's Glen. You can cross the River Gaddagh near a copse of trees where the path and the river diverge. Continue along the path on the far bank of the river to Cronin's Yard.

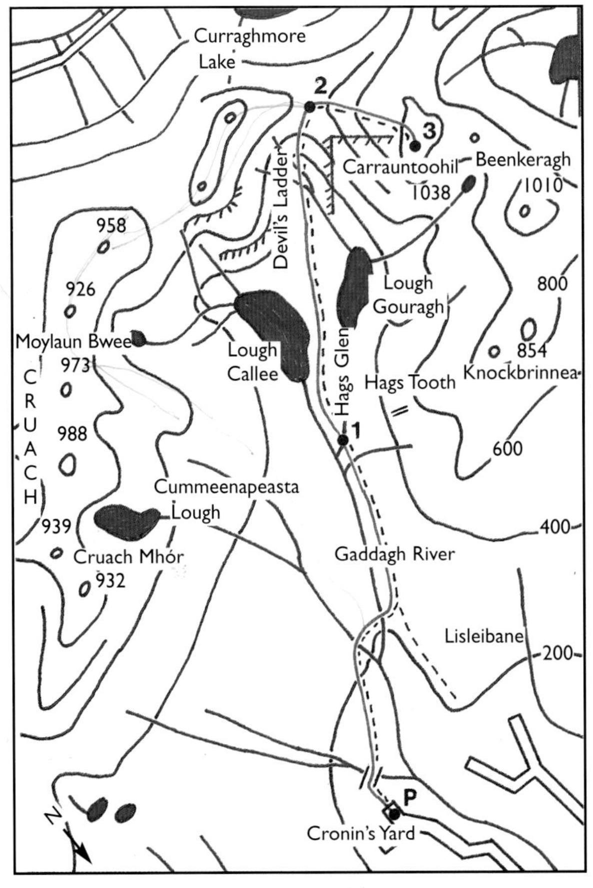

Moderate; 6 hours; 12 kilometres; 900-metre ascent

8 Coomloughra Horseshoe

P–1

Cross the timber fence and climb the steep concreted path into the hills and take in the scenery. Away to the north are the Slieve Mish Mountains, while behind you the bare rock of the Reeks is evident on Skregmore. Follow the path to the bridge and further along you can see that the heather is trying to reclaim the bare scree left after the destruction of the hydroelectric project. Now Caher comes into view as you arrive beside Lough Eighter and the magnificent natural amphitheatre of Coomloughra.

1–2

From the Lough you can clearly see Beenkeragh, Beenkeragh Ridge, Carrauntoohil, and the three high peaks of Caher. Note how steep and inaccessible the ridge is. Head south across the bog banks and climb to the gently sloping spur. Pick up the path and head south-east towards Caher. The ground gets progressively steeper and the views increase in majesty as you gain height. Presently you will reach the first cairned summit of Caher's three distinct peaks (975m).

2–3

Head south-east down to the fence. Now climb again beside the steep cliffs until you arrive at the second of Caher's three peaks (1,001m). On your right is the ridge coming up from Curraghmore Lake, to the south-east Curraghmore Lake and, beyond, the Black Valley. Continue on until you arrive at the third and final peak of Caher. From here all the high peaks of Cruach stretch out before you and the cross on the summit of Carrauntoohil is quite visible. A short descent and one final climb will bring you to the summit of Carrauntoohil (1039m).

3–4

Looking north you can plainly see Beenkeragh and the connecting ridge to your left. The initial descent to the ridge is very steep, so you will have to use your hands for support. The ground levels off for a short while above Looking Glass Lake and Shea's Gully. Here the hills open up with a view down to the Hag's Glen and Lough Leane.

Now you must climb, scramble and inch your way across the ridge until you reach the small cairned summit of Beenkeragh (1010m). On the more difficult sections look out for the path lower down on the left-hand side of the ridge.

4–5

Head north-north-west, carefully picking your way down through the steep crags. As you descend the going will get easier. Continue along the centre of the ridge, staying clear of the cliffs to your right and left. As you progress the terrain will open up for a short while. Now climb to the 851-metre mark and continue in an easterly direction to Screig More (848m) and finally to the 747-metre mark.

5–1–P

Now slowly pick your way down through the crags and scree to Lough Eighter and back along the path to your car.

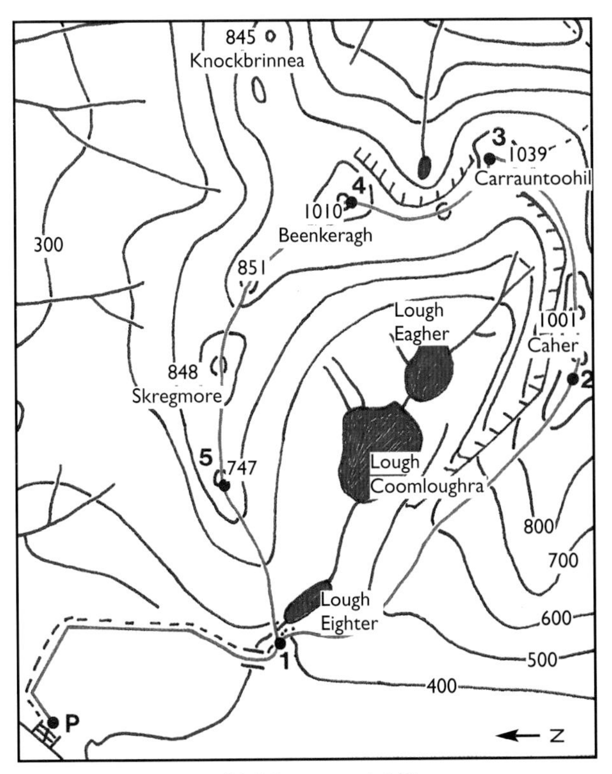

Challenging; 7 hours; 11 kilometres; 1,300-metre ascent

9 Lough Acoose

P–1

With Derryfanga high to your right, continue along the road to the top of the hill and down to Lough Acoose. Take the road on your left beside the Lough. High to your left are Skregmore, Beenkeragh, Carrauntoohil and Caher. Continue on to the top of the hill and the highest point of the walk. From the crest of the hill the road descends towards some farmhouses, and away to your left is a rich patchwork of small fields and stone walls. Past the houses the road continues through a canopy of silver birch trees. The thickness of the stone walls is impressive; the fields were cleared of stones to form the walls. At the junction take the road to the right, cross the bridge and climb towards the farmhouses. At the first derelict building go through and close the gate on your right beside a signpost for the Climber's Inn and the Kerry Way.

1–2

Continue along the path outside the dry stone wall. Here you have fine views of the distant mountains with Lough Beg and Lough Acoose below. The path meanders down to Lough Beg. Climb to the large boulder on the knoll to your left. Behind the boulder is the remnant of a small stone enclosure. From the centre of the enclosure the boulder strangely echoes the shape of the surrounding mountains. Although these large boulders were deposited by glaciers, I sometimes feel they have been placed here on purpose, especially the ones on higher ground. Listen to the noisy stream rushing to enter Lough Beg.

2–3

Climb down to the rushing water, cross the stream and stile.

The path continues on the far side up through the fields, and later above the dry stone wall. Leaving Lough Beg behind, you will soon near the shores of Lough Acoose. Cross the stile, and continue on the path until you arrive at the spot where the water leaves the Lough. Cross the stepping stones near the waters edge and continue on the path to the main road and turn right.

3–P

Now for the first time you get a true feeling for the size of Lough Acoose. Continue on past the memorial to the Irish Volunteers. The road walk is pleasant, with the still waters of Lough Acoose offering a fine mirrored reflection of Caher and the Reeks. So you leave Lough Acoose behind and climb to the top of the hill and back to your car.

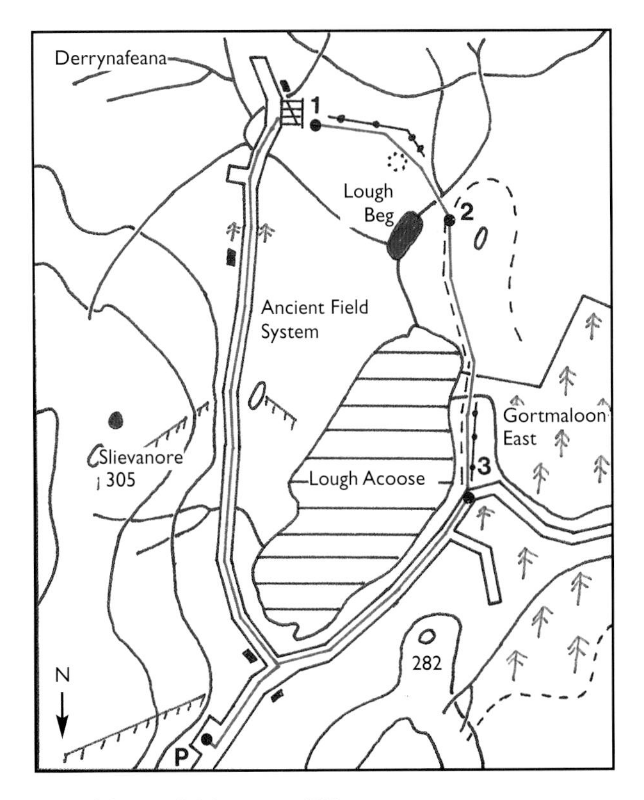

Easy; 3 hours; 6 kilometres; 100-metre ascent

Walk 8, 11 View of Loughs Eagher and Lough Coomloughra in winter

Walk 9 View of Caher reflected in the still waters of Lough Acoose

Walks 10, 11, 12 A derelict cottage in the Black Valley

Walk 10 Lough Reagh and Brassel Mountain

Walk 11 View of Curraghmore Lake and the Macgillycuddy's Reeks

Walk 12 View of Killarney's Upper Lake and Mangerton Mountain

The Black Valley

Despite the large numbers of people who endlessly traipse through the Gap of Dunloe to reach the boats at Lord Brandon's Cottage, relatively few reach the Black Valley and fewer again venture into the hills from this side.

For this reason walks 10,11 and 12 are my favourite. In winter the valley is in shadow and the hills on all sides make for a magical setting. Sadly, the rhododendron, a scourge of the National Park, has taken a foothold in the valley and will prove pandemic if not checked in time.

In contrast to the northern side of the Reeks, where the Hag's Glen is devoid of trees, the Black Valley to the south has small areas of mixed woodland, where mountain ash, alder, silver birch, sessile oak and holly are common.

10 Broaghnabinnia

A strenuous 7 hour, 12 kilometre ridge walk, with a 1,060-metre climb and one particularly steep ascent to Broaghnabinnia. Try to find the Ogham Stone near the start of the walk and spend a little time at the waterfall.

11 Curraghmore

A challenging 7 hour, 12 kilometre ridge walk, with a 1,200-metre climb and one short but severe scramble. Great views into the Black Valley and the Hag's Glen. For safety reasons, don't be tempted into descending the Devil's Ladder or take any short cuts into the Black Valley.

12 Brassel Mountain

A moderate 6 hour, 10 kilometre ridge walk, with 950 metres of ascent and spectacular views of the Black Valley and the Hag's Glen.

10 Broaghnabinnia

P–1

Cross the bridge and head westward through the tubular gate. Now take the path on your left through the corrugated sheep pens and holly trees. Head south across the meadow, cross the river and climb up through the ferns towards the waterfall. Head for the rocky outcrop and continue on to the large split boulder with the heather top.

1–2

Head south-east and pick your way up through the grassy boulder-strewn slope to the summit of Knocknabreeda. This is the only approach to the ridge in an unbroken line of cliffs.

Follow the fence on the boggy plateau towards the amphitheatre above Lough Duff. Here you can see Kenmare Bay, Lough Fadda and Knocklomena to the south. Continue your steep ascent as the ridge narrows, with severe drops to your right and gentler slopes to your left. Contour clockwise near the brow of the hill above Lough Brin.

2–3

Take care while descending from 776m and head north along the spur to 665m. Here you can see Lough Acoose and Inch Strand on the Dingle Peninsula to the north-west.

Head eastward down along the spur through the boulders and rocky outcrops to the col below Broaghnabinnia. These boulders have been here since the last Ice Age and will probably remain where they are until the end of the next.

From the col climb east-north-eastwards on the grassy incline between the rocky outcrops. Turn north, ascending the steep spongy heather-covered slope. Pick the small blueberries, or fraughans, in summer and zigzag your way to the summit.

From the summit of Broaghnabinnia, a 2-kilometre wide coomb and a near vertical 500-metre drop to the valley below offers a magnificent perspective of the northern flank of the Reeks. From here you can clearly see Curraghmore Lake nestling below the three peaks of Caher and the three scarred paths leading to the cross on the summit of Carrauntoohil.

3–P
Now head eastward, staying on the higher section of the ridge, with steep slopes to your right and left. Slowly descend on the steep grass-covered slope to the lower section of the hill. Here you can see the purple scree on Purple Mountain and Killarney's Upper Lake in the distance.

Head for the northern side of the mountain facing Curraghmore Lake and Carrauntoohil. Study the terrain and look for a safe route down beside the stream to the yellow and white houses. Zigzag from left to right and slowly pick your way down to the houses in the valley below.

Cross the river and join the road eastward, back along the Kerry Way to your cars. The road meanders pleasantly down through a line of holly trees, with the waterfall above Lough Reagh just visible in the distance.

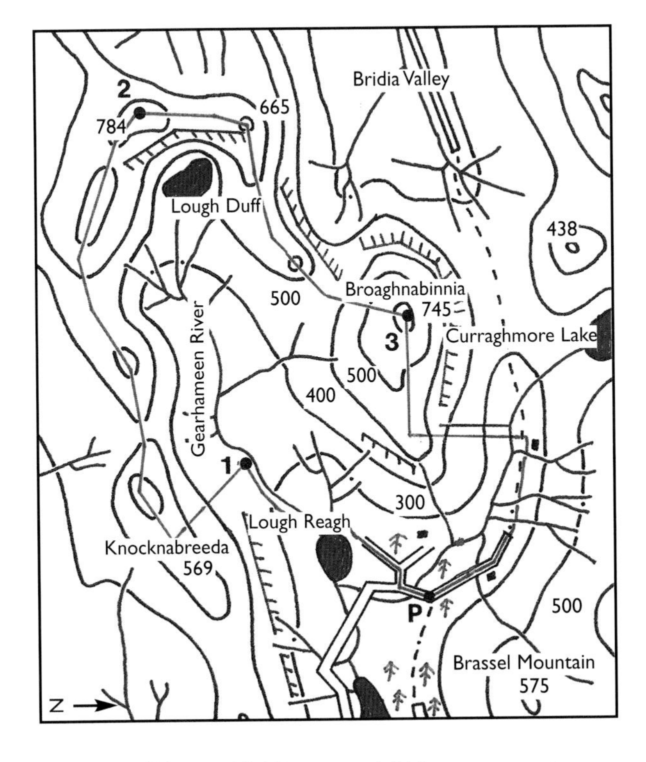

Strenuous; 7 hours; 12 kilometres; 1,060-metre ascent

11 Curraghmore

P–1
Take the road west and contour up the hill, past the derelict house towards the high ridge of Caher and the river below Curraghmore Lake. With Broaghnabinnia high on your left, continue on the Kerry Way through the large gates and on past the yellow house. Continue on beside the stream until the paths diverge and follow the fence up the hill. Follow the grassy path beside the fence, cross the stile and climb the river bank to Curraghmore Lake.

1–2
Continue north-westwards towards the back of the lake and the streams flowing into it. The ground is very boggy, in keeping with the lake's name.

Head westward beside the stream, climbing through the boulder fields towards the domed outcrop of Curraghmore.

Approaching the outcrop look for the fence away to your left, and climb beside the fence until it ends under a rocky face.

Now climb in a north-westerly direction up the screed slope, hugging the side of the hill. Cross the stone wall and continue to scramble your way up to level ground below the sheer cliffs of Caher's Ridge.

Stop and take in the scenery and then follow the path over to your left and up the screed slope beside the stream under the sheer rock face. Slowly climb and scramble your way towards the grassy ridge, using your hands extensively as you near the summit of Curraghmore.

2–3
Head north along the ridge, climbing towards the second of Caher's three peaks, with fine views of Curraghmore Lake and the yellow house below to your right.

Continue in an easterly direction, with Lough Coomloughra and Lough Eagher to your left. The path along the ridge is well defined with a sheer precipice on your left and steep slopes on your right. Continue to the third of Caher's peaks. With the knife-edged ridge of Beenkeragh straight ahead, one final descent remains before you make the short climb to the summit of Carrauntoohil. Rest and touch the cross for luck before you proceed.

3–4

Head south and descend the cairn-strewn path to the col above the Devil's Ladder. Climb again to the wide grass-covered plateau, where you can amble along at your ease.

To your left are the Hag's Glen, Lough Callee and Lough Gouragh. Now descend to the fence and on to the col before climbing the scree-strewn path to Foilnagower (958m).

4–P

Head south-east down the steep, broad-backed grassy slope towards the col below Brassel Mountain. You may find the going easier near the fencing on your left.

Head south-west towards Broaghnabinnia and down the gully, where the constant pouring of water has rounded and blackened the rocks. Continue your descent until you reach the line of ferns. Now cross into the boulder fields on your left and continue down to the road and to your car.

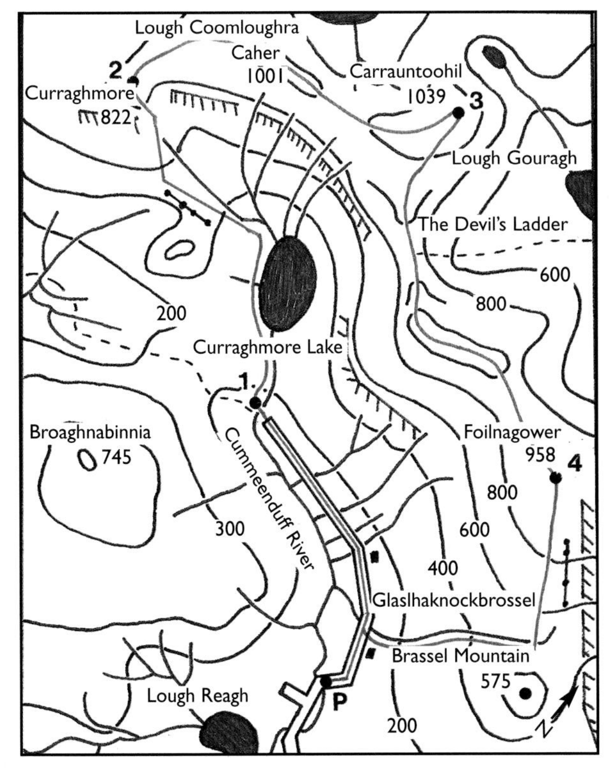

Challenging; 7 hours; 12 kilometres; 1,200-metre ascent

12 Brassel Mountain

P–1

Head west along the road, with Brassel Mountain on your right and mixed woodland on your left. Continue on to the derelict house with the hawthorn trees and ivy-covered slate roof.

Head north-eastward towards Brassel Mountain, climbing up through the gorse reeds and boulders and on to the dry stone wall. The large boulders are covered in a rich mosaic of colourful lichens silently conducting chemical warfare with each other. Look back and take in the patchwork of woods and small fields below. Gaining height, climb beside the fence to the summit of Brassel Mountain (575m). The summit is flat, with no individual peak to offer a view of the surrounding hills.

1–2

Here you can see the fence and the black scar of rocks with water flowing down the mountainside from the ridge above. Cross the fence and continue on down to the col. To the east are Torc Mountain and Killarney's Upper Lake with the river Duff slowly meandering out through the Black Valley.

Climb beside the fence until it ends beside a large rocky outcrop. Head west to the stream and climb the steep grassy slope between the rocky outcrops. Slowly zigzag your way to the ridge between Foilnagower and Ballaghnageeha.

2–3

Here you can see the high peaks of Carrauntoohil and Beenkeragh, with Lough Callee and Lough Gouragh in the Hag's Glen. Head east along the path to Ballaghnageeha (926m) with the jagged profile of the Bone below Moylaun Bwee on your left. With sheer precipices to your right and left, continue on the ridge to the small cairn on Moylaun Bwee (973m). The ridge is flat and grass-covered. Continue on towards the rock-strewn scree margin at the base of the Lackagarriv (988m).

3–4

Contour slowly eastward on the hill until you see Lough Googh. Now head south-eastward down the centre of the steep grassy spur, with cliffs on your left and steeper areas to your right towards Feabrahy.

As you descend, take in the spectacular views down to the Black Valley and the ruggedness of Brassel Mountain. Away to the north-east beyond Lough Googh you can clearly see the East Peak and Bull Mountain, with its scattering of large boulders.

Head south-south-west and slowly descend the rock-strewn slope, contouring around the bluffs of rock. Continue on to the river flowing from Lough Calee and follow the fence down the right bank. Make your way south through the fields, using the gates, until you reach the road beyond.

4–P

Turn right and follow the road on the Kerry Way to the forest and on through the boulder fields. Cross the fence and continue on the path until you reach the road and head downhill through the avenue of holly trees to your car.

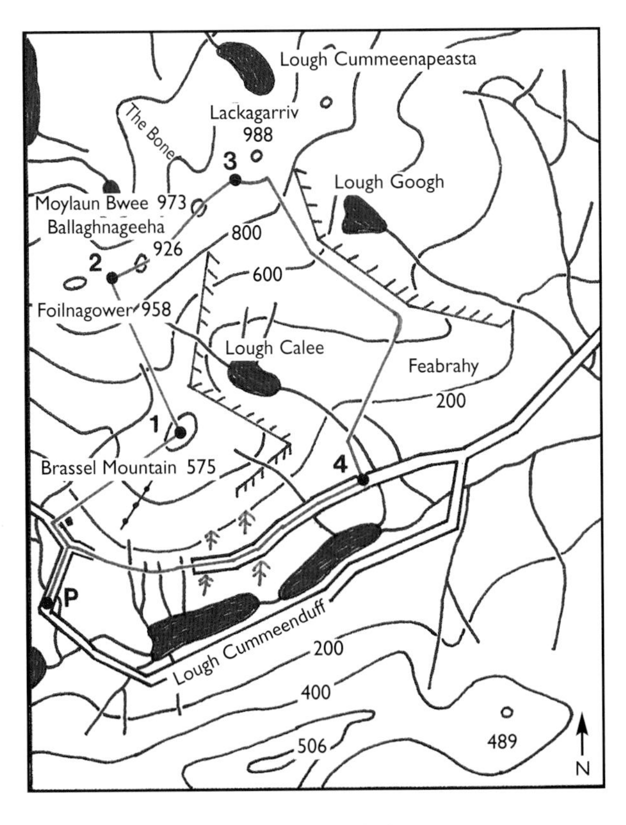

Moderate; 6 hours; 10 kilometres; 950-metre ascent

Meaning of Irish Place Names

Mountains, Hills, Peaks

Beenkeragh	Binn Chaorach	peak of the sheep
Brassel	Breasail	hill/willow tree
Brickeen Bridge	Droichead Bricín	bridge/small trout
Broaghnabinnia	Bruach na Binne	edge of the peak
Caher	Cathair	fortress
Carrauntoohil	Corrán Tuathail	left handed sickle
Coomclochan	Coomclachan	stony glen
Derryfanga	Derryfanga	sloping oak woods
Drishana	Drisean	place of brambles
Dromluska	Drom luachair	ridge of rushes
Gap of Dunloe	Bearna an Choimí	gap in the hills
Gortadirra	Gortadoire	field/oak-grove
Knocklomena	Cnoc an Mheannáin	hill/pinnacled cliff
Knocknabreeda	Cnoc na Breeda	hill of Bridget
	Cnoc na Tarbh	hill of the bull
Macgillycuddy	Mac-gilly-cuddy	son/servant/Cuddy
Purple	An Sliabh Corcra	a pointed hill
Shehy	Cnoc Seithe	hill of the fairies
Skregbeg	Screig Bheag	small rocky hill
Skregmore	Screig Mhór	large rocky hill
Strickeen	Struicín	top of the bog
Tomies	Na Toimi	burial mound

Six Peaks of Cruach

Peaks of Cruach	Na Cruacha Dubha	the black peaks
932 metres	Cruach Mhór	a large peak, rick
939 metres	Foilnabreachaun	cliff of the crows
988 metres	Lackagarriv	a rough flagstone
973 metres	Moylaun Bwee	bold yellow hill
926 metres	Ballaghnageeha	pass of the winds
958 metres	Foilnagower	cliff of the goats

Rivers and Streams

Gaddagh	an Gheadach	rough bedded
Gearhameen	Ghaortnaidh Mhín	gentle windy river

Lough, Loch and Lakes

Acoose	Dhá Chuais	two caves
Auger	Auger	stony bedded
Beg	Beag	small
Brin	Braín	hill
Callee	Caillí	the hags
Coomloughra	ChomLuachra	glen of rushes
Coosaun	an Chuasáin	a small cave

Cushvally	Cushnavally	foot of the valley
Cummeenapeasta	Cuimmin-na-peiste	serpents hollow
Cummeenduff	Cummeenduff	small black hollow
Cummeenmore	Coimín Mór	large hollow
Curraghmore	An Currach Mór	a large bog
Duff	Dú Loch	black
Eagher	Iarthair	western
Eighter	Iochtair	lower
Fada	Fada	long
Glas	Glas	grey-green
Gouragh	Gabhrach	goats
Googh	gCuach	bowl shaped hollow
Leane	Léin	smooth
Looscaunagh	Luascánaigh	bald rushes
Muckross	Mhucrois	pig grove
Reagh	Riabhach	grey-streaked
Upper	Uachtarach	upper

Towns, Villages, Townlands

Beaufort	Lios na Phúca	fort of the fairies
Fossa	Fossa	a fort
Kenmare	Neidín	little nest
Killarney	Cill Airne	church of the sloes
Meallis	Meallis	a bare place
Rossbeigh	Ros Beithe	headland of birches

Getting Started (with Grid References)

There is nothing more infuriating for hillwalkers than wasting precious time driving down endless small roads with no apparent access to the hills. The following pages should make this task an easy one. Use the grid references provided to find the 6 starting points for the 12 walks on the Ordnance Survey map.

Walk 1 Muckross Lake (950 847)

From Killarney take the Muckross Road (N71) south for 8 kilometres to Muckross Lake. Park your car in the lay-by on your right beside the lake and the entrance to Killarney National Park. Before starting out, study the local map in the car park.

Walk 2 Tomies Wood (896 902)

From Killarney take the Killorglin Road (N72) westward for 6 kilometres to the village of Fossa. Now take the next road on your left, signposted for the Gap of Dunloe. After 3 kilometres the road swings sharply to the right. Here take the small road on your left signposted for Lough Leane and park your car before the bridge near the signpost for Tomies Wood.

Walks 3, 4 Kate Kearney's Cottage (881 888)

From Killarney take the Killorglin Road (N72) westward for 9 kilometres to Beaufort Bridge. Head over the bridge and through the village of Beaufort to the crossroads. Continue south towards the Gap of Dunloe, parking your car outside Kate Kearney's Cottage.

Walks 5, 6, 7 Cronin's Yard (836 873)

From Killarney take the (Killorglin Road N72) for 9 kilometres to Beaufort Bridge. Head south over the bridge and through the village of Beaufort to the crossroads. Now head west for 4 kilometres to Kissane's Cross.

Cross the bridge and take the small road on your left signposted for Carrauntoohil. As you drive along the narrow pot-holed road into the hills, the whole panorama of the Reeks and Carrauntoohil opens up before you. You can park in the cul-de-sac at Cronin's Yard for a small consideration. Even from a distance of 4 kilometres Carrauntoohil is still dominant.

Walks 8, 9 Near Lough Acoose (771 870)

From Killarney take the Killorglin Road (N72) for 9 kilometres to Beaufort Bridge. Head south over the bridge through the village of Beaufort to the crossroads. Now head west for a further 14 kilometres, skirting the base of the Reeks. Gradually the road turns south as you continue to climb into the hills. Park near the timber gate and fence on your left.For walk 9 continue on to the top of the hill and park your car in the large lay-by on your left. (763 864)

Walks 10, 11, 12 The Black Valley (822 815)

From Killarney take the Kenmare Road (N71) for 20 kilometres into the hills to Moll's Gap.Turn right and take the small road on your right signposted for the Black Valley. Continue on for 12 kilometres to the lakes and park your car on the grassy verge on your left beyond the third bridge.You can also take a shorter 15 kilometre drive through the Gap of Dunloe to the Black Valley. The road narrows near the Head of the Gap and is in a bad state of repair from the jarvies' horses and their carts.

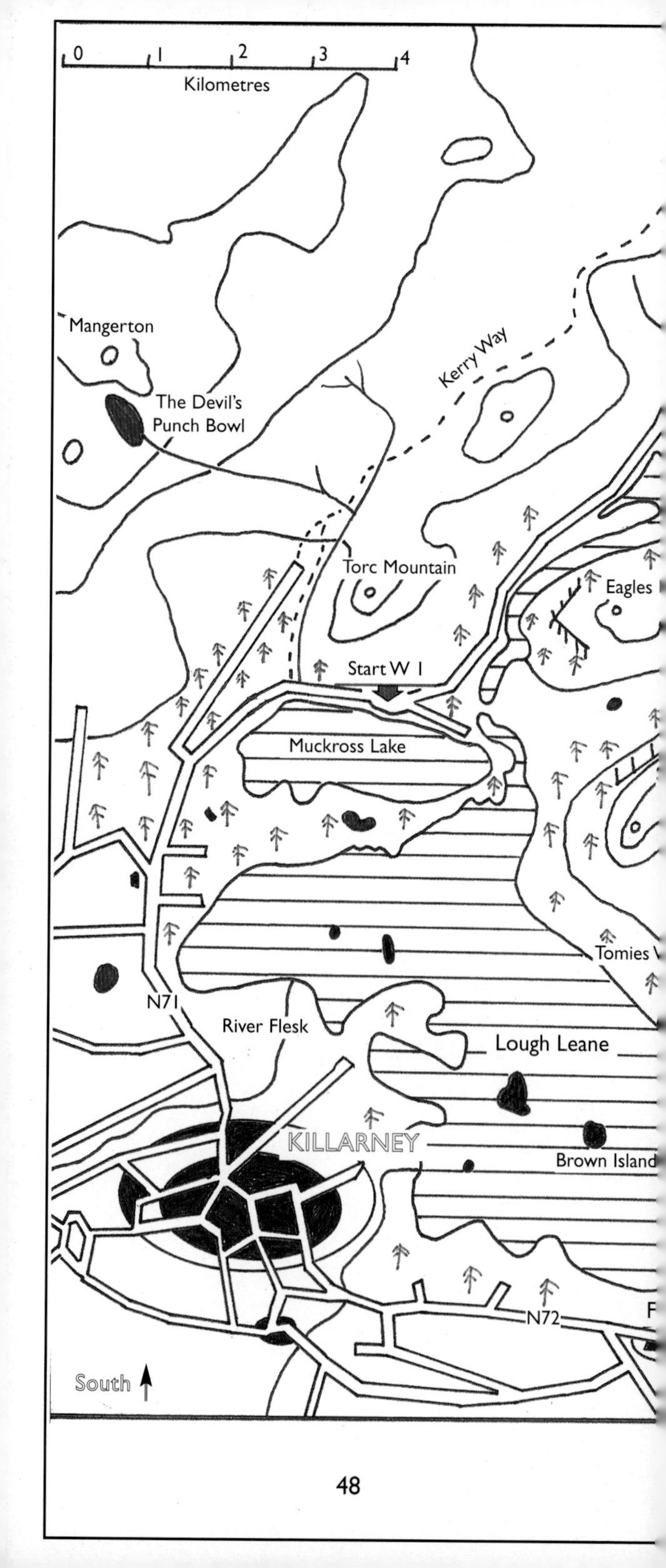
0
1
2
3
4
Kilometres
Mangerton
The Devil's Punch Bowl
Kerry Way
Torc Mountain
Eagles
Start W 1
Muckross Lake
Tomies
N71
River Flesk
Lough Leane
KILLARNEY
Brown Island
N72
South